SCHIRMER
PERFORMANCE
EDITIONS

LABORUM
DULCE
LENIMEN

G. SCHIRMER

HAL LEONARD PIANO LIBRARY

# KABALEVSKY

## SELECTED PIANO PIECES

### Intermediate Level

17 Pieces from Various Opus Sets
in Progressive Order

Compiled and Edited by Richard Walters

Some pieces were previously published in the following
Schirmer Performance Editions volumes:

*Kabalevsky: 30 Pieces for Children*, Op. 27
edited by Richard Walters

*Kabalevsky: 24 Pieces for Children*, Op. 39
edited by Margaret Otwell

*The 20th Century: Intermediate Level*
edited by Richard Walters

On the cover:
*Color Study: Squares with Concentric Circles* (1913)
by Wassily Kandinsky (1866–1944)

ISBN 978-1-4950-8883-4

## G. SCHIRMER, Inc.

DISTRIBUTED BY
HAL•LEONARD®
7777 W. BLUEMOUND RD. P.O. BOX 13819 MILWAUKEE, WI 53213

www.musicsalesclassical.com
**www.halleonard.com**

# CONTENTS

*Though presented by opus number on the table contents,*
*the music is presented in progressive order of difficulty*

# HISTORICAL NOTES

## DMITRI KABALEVSKY (1904–1987)

"Art shapes the man, his heart and mind, his feelings and convictions—the whole of his spiritual world. More than that art influences the development of society." —Dmitri Kabalevsky

Kabalevsky was born in St. Petersburg the son of a mathematician. Dmitri not only learned to play the piano, but also was a competent poet and painter as well. Facing financial difficulties, the family moved to Moscow following the October Revolution of 1917. Economic conditions in Russia were dire following World War I. In the ensuing political upheaval, work was hard to find. The Kabalevskys struggled as part of the working poor. Dmitri assisted in bringing in income, beginning to give piano lessons at 15 and playing for silent films at the theatre. He also held odd jobs, including delivering mail and drawing placards for shop windows.

In 1918, Kabalevsky began studying piano and art at the Scriabin Institute. His father wanted him to focus on economics and become a mathematician, but music quickly won the young boy's passions. He soon began teaching at the institute. Kabalevsky enrolled at the Moscow Conservatory in 1925, studying composition and piano.

At the conservatory Kabalevsky joined two musical groups. The Proizvodstvennyi Kollektiv was a conservative, pro-Lenin organization. The Association of Contemporary Musicians was a progressive, avant-garde group. Hardly ten years after the Revolution and the uncertainty of political stability, Kabalevsky deliberately formed relationships with both political camps. This diplomacy would make him one of the most powerful musical voices in the USSR.

Kabalevsky graduated from the conservatory in 1930 and began lecturing there soon after. In 1932, when the Communist Party dissolved all music organizations and created the Union of Soviet Composers, Kabalevsky stepped up as a founding member, using his ties with the more conservative

Proizvodstvennyi Kollektiv to demonstrate his commitment to traditional Russian values and the Russian people. He became a writer for the magazine *Muzgiz* and for *Moscow Radio*. These platforms allowed him to endorse Russian music that was "for the people" and condemn the music that was overly "formalist," a catch-all phrase used by Communist leaders to identify art intended for the "intellectual connoisseurs or sophisticated esoterics," ideas the Communists lifted almost directly from Tolstoy's *What is Art?*

Kabalevsky married in 1931, divorced in 1935, and remarried in 1937. During this time, in addition to his continued teaching appointment at the Moscow Conservatory, he became the senior editor of *Muzgiz*. In 1939, he gained full professorship at the conservatory. Throughout the 1930s, Kabalevsky began to take a more prominent role in the Union of Soviet Composers and in the 1940s, became editor of the *Sovetskaya Muzika*, as well as the Chief of the Board of Feature Broadcasting on *Moscow Radio* after joining the Communist Party. The Soviet government considered him important enough to be evacuated during World War II to Sverdlovsk (now Yekaterinburg) as Hitler's army drew closer to Moscow.

Following World War II, the Conference of Musicians at the Central Committee of the All-Union Communist Party was held in 1948 to outline a policy known as Socialist Realism, the official name of Marxist art and aesthetic theory. The policy asked artists to create art that is "comprehensible to the masses, and inspires the people with admiration for the dignity of the working man and his task of building Communism."[1] The conference and ensuing policy spawned widespread questioning of anyone whose music was not politically correct. There were interrogations and threats to those who would not change their style to serve the party. Somehow Kabalevsky managed to get his name removed from the list of potentially "harmful" composers. He is the only prominent Russian composer of the time to avoid interrogation.

Kabalevsky published just over 100 pieces and wrote far more during his life. Most famous today are his suite *The Comedians*, his violin concerto, and several piano collections. The style is always conservative, approachable, and clear, yet quirky, inventive, and light-hearted. Kabalevsky's music demonstrates a master composer capable of disciplined and limited use of material based on a few fundamentals, like a painter that deliberately uses a limited palate of colors.

Beginning in the 1950s until his death, Kabalevsky wrote little music. Instead, he became heavily involved in national and international pedagogical organizations. From 1952 until his death he served on the board of the Union of Soviet Composers of the USSR; in 1953 he became a member of the Soviet Committee for the Defense of Peace; in 1954, USSR Ministry of Culture; in 1955, World Peace Council; in 1961, United Nations Educational, Scientific and Cultural Organization International Music Council, Council of Directors of the International Society for Music Education. Later, he became a member of the Committee for Lenin Prizes for Literature and Art, the Head of the Council on Aesthetic Education, a deputy to the USSR Supreme Council, Honorary President of the Academy of Pedagogical Sciences in the USSR, and Honorary President of the International Society of Music Education.

During much of this time, Kabalevsky also gave lectures on radio, television, and at various functions in many different countries on music appreciation, pedagogy, and aesthetics.

Perhaps Kabalevsky's most enduring contribution to Soviet music education was his work with the Laboratory of Musical Education in the 1970s. He succeeded in compiling specific lesson plans to be implemented in all Soviet classrooms. It became a complete syllabus (texts, recordings, and detailed outlines of each lesson) for all music education

in the country. He then went into the primary schools of Moscow to implement this system. The program focused on political indoctrination, moral education, and character training at its base. Eventually Kabalevsky retired from the conservatory and dedicated his full attention to the education of children in primary schools. He stated in 1974, "when I decided it was time to sum up my work in this [music education] field, I discovered that it was not the summing up, but the beginning of a new stage. I realized that all I had done was merely preparation for going into general schools not merely as a composer or lecturer, but as an ordinary teacher of music."[2]

Up to the last moments of his life Kabalevsky was furthering music education and peaceful relations between all people of all cultures. He died of a heart attack at a conference at which he was to deliver a lecture on the disarmament of world powers of their nuclear weapons.

In Frank Callaway's eulogy given a few days later, he summed up the great influence of the composer: "Kabalevsky believed and demonstrated that music cultivates the artistic tastes and the creative imagination of children, as well as their love of life, of people, of nature, of motherland, and fosters their interest in, and friendships toward, peoples of all nations."[3]

[1] David Lawrence Forrest, *The Educational Theory of Dmitri Kabalevsky in Relation to His Piano Music for Children* (Ph.D. diss., University of Melbourne. 1996), 87.

[2] ibid., 36.

[3] ibid., 40.

# INTRODUCTION TO KABALEVSKY'S MUSIC

"We live in a difficult—interesting but difficult—epoch, but still life is wonderful. Great art can only come from love for life, love for man. Art must serve society, the people must understand it. The love of man must be there." —Dmitri Kabalevsky.[1]

In his book *Music and Education: A Composer Writes About Musical Education*, Kabalevsky several times cites the quotation by Maxim Gorki that books for children should be "the same as for adults, only better."[2] This quotation is the guiding principle behind all of Kabalevsky's music for children. He did not want to compose simplified or dumbed-down adult art, but good art for children. This flowed very naturally out of his educational theories, that of teaching musical literacy rather than musical grammar, instructing how to listen to music, define shapes and structures, not just how to read or how to identify elements of music.

Building an educational framework, Kabalevsky's book *A Story of Three Whales and Many Other Things* identifies three archetypes as basic musical forms from which all other larger forms are generated and most accessible to children: song, dance, and march. The archetypes (or whales) become the bridges upon which children may enter the world of music. Nearly all of Kabalevsky's music for children can be understood as fitting into one of these categories.

Kabalevsky believed that "no piece of music, however short and modest, should pass by a child without touching his mind and heart."[3] And it is easy to hear in his pedagogical works that he was focusing on developing a real musical understanding in children rather than just getting them to practice or learn scales.

Kabalevsky composed 253 pieces during his lifetime. There are 26 sonatas, sets or suites of piano music, from concert level works for advanced players to 153 pieces specifically written for progressing piano students. It is no wonder he has remained such a popular choice among piano teachers.

It is worth saying that Kabalevsky considered music to be for people of all ages. His specific emphasis was on creating good music first, then helping students understand the music. Even though some of the titles of his works refer to children, they continue in the tradition established by composers like Schumann and Tchaikovsky in creating well-crafted, approachable pieces that focus on specific pedagogical techniques that piano students of any age will find valuable.

[1] in an interview with *The New York Times*, October 27, 1957 "Optimistic Russian: Kabalevsky, in Speaking of His Fourth Symphony, Reveals Attitude to Life" (quoted in Forrest, 103).

[2] Dmitri Kabalevsky, *Music and Education: A Composer Writes About Musical Education* (London: Jessica Kingsley Publishers, 1988), 120.

[3] David Lawrence Forrest, *The Educational Theory of Dmitri Kabalevsky in Relation to His Piano Music for Children* (Ph.D. diss., University of Melbourne. 1996), 143.

## References

Daragan, Dina Grigor'yevna. "Kabalevsky, Dmitry Borisovich," *The New Grove Dictionary of Music and Musicians*. ed. S. Sadie and J. Tyrrell. London: Macmillan. 2001.

Forrest, David Lawrence. *The Educational Theory of Dmitri Kabalevsky in Relation to His Piano Music for Children*. (Ph.D. diss., University of Melbourne. 1996).

Kabalevsky, Dimitri. *Music and Education: A Composer Writes About Musical Education*. London: Jessica Kingsley Publishers, 1988.

Krebs, Stanley Dale. *Soviet Composers and the Development of Soviet Music*. New York: W. W. Norton & Company, 1970.

Maes Francis. trans. Arnold J. and Erica Pomerans. *A History of Russian Music: From Kamarinskaya to Babi Yar*. Berkley: University of California Press, 2002.

—Richard Walters, editor
and Joshua Parman, assistant editor

# ABOUT THE INDIVIDUAL PIECES
## in order by opus number

*24 Pieces for Children*, Op. 39 is similar to *35 Easy Pieces*, Op. 89, composed almost 30 years later. Both sets start with beginner level pieces and move progressively up to what could be called an early intermediate level. 30 Pieces for Children, Op. 27, begins at a bit higher level, probably what could generally be called early intermediate, and progresses up to upper intermediate or slightly beyond.

The pieces in *From the Life of a Pioneer*, Op. 14 are certainly for students, and seem a warm-up for Op. 27, composed a few years later. Also written for students, composed with didactic purpose, are *Easy Variations*, Op. 51, *Four Easy Rondos*, Op. 60, *Six Preludes & Fugues*, Op. 61, and *Six Pieces* (Children's Dreams), Op. 88.

The *Four Preludes*, Op. 5 and *24 Preludes*, Op. 38 are more decidedly concert material, not didactic in the spirit of the "children's pieces," and more harmonically adventurous. We have chosen a few pieces from these, still at intermediate level, to deepen the representation of the composer in this volume.

### Prelude in A minor from *Four Preludes*, Op. 5, No. 1
composed 1927–28

*Practice and Performance Tips*
- Kabalevsky's articulations (especially those notes with *tenuto* markings) are a clue to where the voice in the texture should be most prominent.
- A major challenge of this work is managing the sound between the various voices.
- It may take practice over time to make sense of this piece. Follow the dynamic markings, the articulations, and the changes in tempo Kabalevsky has written to shape it.
- The climax is in measures 11–12, with an *accelerando* and *crescendo* leading to it.
- This plaintive music asks for sensitive musicality.
- Carefully listen as you use the pedal, keeping the harmonies clear.

### Sporting Game from *From Pioneer Life*, Op. 14, No. 2
composed 1931

*Practice and Performance Tips*
- Because the hands are so interconnected, this piece is probably easier to practice hands together, slowly, rather than hands separately.
- Typical of Kabalevsky, almost every note has an articulation or slur related to it. These are extremely important in realizing an effective performance.
- Notice the *tenuto* marking under beat 1 in the first measure. This indicates the notes are to be played with emphasis, held to the notes' full value. It would be easy to smack this and make it too short. This same rhythmic figure recurs several times.
- A tricky spot is measure 38, where the pattern changes from what is expected.
- Keep a steady tempo as you practice, and as you become more comfortable, increase the tempo. The ultimate final performance tempo should be fairly quick and playful (*scherzando* means joking).
- Use no sustaining pedal.

### Selections from *30 Pieces for Children*, Op. 27
composed 1937–38 (slightly revised 1985)

#### Etude in A minor (No. 3)
*Practice and Performance Tips*
- This piece is a scale study. It would be good to practice A-minor scales along with it.
- Practice hands alone, slowly at first.
- Keep the sixteenth notes very steady and even in the right hand.
- Increase tempo speed, retaining steadiness, in the right hand alone as you practice. Any unevenness in scale technique will be readily apparent.
- The left hand must be very steady. Also note the composer's two-note slurs and specific pedal markings.
- When finally moving to hands together practice, start slowly. This piece should begin at a practice tempo that will be quite a bit slower than the final performance tempo.

- The piece will be dull if you do not pay attention to the composer's dynamics, which provide much contrast.
- In places such as measures 1–3, notice the feeling of quick up and down swells ("hairpins").
- Even though in a minor key, it feels light-heartedly menacing.
- Strive for steady evenness and fluidity rather than speed, paying attention to all details of dynamics, pedaling and articulation.

## A Little Prank (No. 13)

*Practice and Performance Tips*
- The title indicates playfulness, and the composer gives unexpected twists in the harmony.
- Divide the piece into three sections for practice. section 1: measures 1–16; section 2: pickup to measure 17–33; section 3: measures 34–53.
- Begin practice slowly, hands together.
- The descending five-finger scales in the right hand need to be played with crystal clear evenness.
- Note the composer's marking of *leggiero*, which means lightly.
- The music relies on its articulation; note the slurring and *staccato* markings.
- Use absolutely no sustaining pedal.
- Most students will need to give measures 20–22 and 28–30 special attention. Practice these hands separately, then hands together slowly.
- Gradually increase your practice tempo over time, but always keeping a steady beat.

## Lyric Piece (No. 16)

*Practice and Performance Tips*
- As might be guessed of music titled "Lyric Piece," it is primarily about song-like melody.
- The right-hand melody should predominate over the left-hand accompaniment in measures 3–12.
- The melody moves to the left hand in measures 12–17, before returning to the right hand in measure 17.
- Practice the melody, noted above, separately, aiming to create a smooth and musically pleasing line, using the phrasing that Kabalevsky has composed to shape the melody.

- The melancholy spirit, combined with the long melody, is reminiscent of Chopin.
- Pedaling is explicitly marked by the composer. Practice the left hand alone with the pedaling.
- The composer takes the music into unexpected harmony in measure 17, then again in measure 21.
- Except for the opening motive, which returns at the end of measure 31, this is quiet music, marked *p*. Do not allow it to bloom too far past that quiet dynamic.

## Fairy Tale (No. 20)

*Practice and Performance Tips*
- A fairy tale story might take unusual, unexpected twists, but there is always a happy ending. This music captures that.
- Practice slowly hands separately.
- For the right hand, get very well acquainted with the melody, its shape, and Kabalevsky's expressive dynamics and articulations.
- In practicing the left hand alone, aim for absolute evenness, steadiness and smoothness. Note the constant four-note phrasing, with the pedal always changing on beat 3.
- In the left hand the four eighth notes (always three down then one up) outline a triad or a seventh chord. It may help to memorize to grasp the chord being outlined.
- The repeated notes in measure 1 and in similar places are an important part of the texture. The composer does not state it, but it feels possible to add a bit of a swell into the second measure of this figure.
- The tempo, *andantino cantabile*, is a clear signal that this music is about the singing right-hand melody.
- Even though pedaling is used throughout, you should practice without pedal to achieve clarity of touch, tone, and evenness.

## The Chase (No. 21)

*Practice and Performance Tips*
- Most pieces with "chase" in the title have one hand following the other. This is not the case here. The hands play in octaves throughout.
- Practice hands separately, slowly. For most students, getting the left hand as fluent as the right will be the challenge.
- It will help you learn the piece to learn the articulation from the beginning, when practicing hands separately.

- Begin practice, slowly, hands together. Listen to hear if the left hand is matching the right hand exactly. A lack of evenness between hands will be very exposed. If the left hand is lazy, it will be very apparent to any listener.
- The articulation is exactly the same for both hands.
- The music has a fleeting texture and must be played with a nimble touch.
- No pedaling; it would be against the character and inappropriate.
- The music falls very easily under the hands once it has been learned.
- Over time, increase practice speed, always remaining steady.
- A tricky spot is measure 17. Take care with fingering here.

### Novelette (No. 25)

*Practice and Performance Tips*
- Novelette is a title invented by Schumann for his opus 21 for pensive, solemn music that tells a melancholy story.
- Kabalevsky had a story in mind that we cannot discover, but the emotional contour comes through. Kabalevsky might have had words in mind as a compositional tool.
- The left hand is accompaniment, a low sound answered by a mid-range sound in the second half of each measure.
- The right hand plays the melody, almost always doubled in thirds.
- Pedal carefully. Generally, pedal on every downbeat.
- In the right hand, use *legato* fingers wherever possible.

### Selections from *24 Preludes*, Op. 38
composed 1943–44

### Prelude in C Major (No. 1)

*Practice and Performance Tips*
- Unlike Kabalevsky's music for students, this is a concert work in a different style. It will take a little more work to understand and put together.
- Practice hands separately, and learn all the dynamics and articulations as you do.
- When putting hands together in practice, retain all the dynamics and articulations you have already learned when practicing hands separately.

- This is a quiet piece. You might practice at a louder volume to learn the music. Then find a round tone and soft volume after you have mastered it confidently.
- Some pianists will have trouble stretching a tenth in measures 4, 13, 25, and 27. It may be necessary to roll the chords.
- Though Kabalevsky does not provide us with any pedaling instructions, the use of pedaling is almost mandatory. Be careful to change with each harmony so the texture does not become blurred.
- Measures 13–18 are particularly difficult to pedal. Listen carefully to the sound you are producing.
- In measures 9 and 11, the right hand crosses the left. Be sure the audience can hear this counter melody prominently. The right hand crosses the left again in measures 19–21.
- This piece requires sensitive musicality and some maturity as a pianist.

### Prelude in D-flat Major (No. 15)

*Practice and Performance Tips*
- Unlike Kabalevsky's music for students, this is a concert work in a different style. It will take a little more work to understand and put together.
- Independence of hands is a particular challenge in this piece. Careful practice hands alone will be a key in solving this challenge, slowly in the beginning.
- Learning the articulation from the beginning as you practice each hand alone will make the piece easier to grasp.
- Exaggerate the contrasts between *f* and *mf*, and *mf* and *p*.
- The tied A-flat in measures 30–31 might appear confusing at first. This is executed by striking the note with finger 5 in the left hand, and then substituting with finger 1 in the right hand without re-striking the note.
- Increase the tempo as you become more confident. Keep a feeling of "march" and don't press the tempo too much ultimately.
- Probably use no sustaining pedal throughout.

**Slow Waltz from *24 Pieces for Children*, Op. 39, No. 23**

composed 1944

*Practice and Performance Tips*

- Practice hands separately.
- In the right hand practice, pay attention to slurs and staccato marks, and aim for shapely expression.
- In the left hand, practice the wide jumps of hand position (measures 1–2, for instance). They should sound easy and graceful. Note that almost everything in the left hand is marked *staccato*.
- Experiment with tempo when playing hands together. It should be slow, but not too slow.
- Note the composer's marking of *tranquillo* (tranquil) in mood.
- Resist the urge to use the sustaining pedal.
- The performer should observe all the articulations carefully, especially when holding the right-hand notes while simultaneously playing the left-hand notes *staccato*, as in the first two measures.
- Your finished performance should be elegant, with a hint of melancholy.

**Selections from *Five Easy Variations on Folk Themes*, Op. 51**

composed 1952

**Dance Variations on a Russian Folk Song (No. 2)**

*Practice and Performance Tips*

- Practice the theme first, and get to know it very well before moving onto the variations.
- In measures 4 and 8 on beat 2, notice that the right-hand note is held a little longer than the left-hand *staccato* note.
- The eighth notes of the right-hand melody in the theme must be very evenly played.
- In Variation 1 the right hand is smooth and sustained while the left hand continues to play *staccato*.
- Practice Variation 1 hands separately to work on the different articulation in each hand.
- Create nice contrast by playing Variation 1 *p*, as marked.
- Find the character of each individual variation. Practice each separately, so they each emerge as something special, with distinct expression.
- Kabalevsky's dynamics and articulations will help you find the character of each variation.
- The right-hand moving notes in Variation 5 and the left-hand moving notes in Variation 6

will need obvious practice attention. Aim for flowing evenness.
- It would be alright to pause (only slightly) between variations.

**Seven Cheerful Variations on a Slovakian Folk Song (No. 4)**

*Practice and Performance Tips*

- As with learning any theme and variations, it's very important to get to know the theme extremely well so that you can emphasize what the composer is doing with the theme in each variation.
- Practice the right-hand theme alone ensuring all notes are even, that all *staccatos* are the same length, and that there is direction and purpose to the shape of the melody. Remember that *scherzando* means joking.
- Learn each variation one at a time, separately and distinctly. Give each careful practice.
- Sometimes the tempo changes in a set of variations. That's not the case in this set. The initial *allegretto* holds steady throughout.
- Practice each variation hands separately. Learning the articulation as you learn the notes will make things easier in the long run.
- Kabalevsky composed so many colorful details of articulation and dynamics along with the notes. Mastering those is as important as mastering the notes and rhythms. They are part of the composition, not something added to it.

**Selections from *Four Rondos*, Op. 60**

composed 1958

**Rondo-Song (No. 3)**

*Practice and Performance Tips*

- The rondo theme is the melody in the right hand in measures 1–12. This recurs in the left hand in measures 21–30, and again in the right hand in measures 49–59.
- Practice hands separately. This will help with the trickiest spots, such as measures 30–31.
- Pay careful attention to Kabalevsky's slurs and phrases, and shape your playing with those as a guide.
- The pedaling is very specific, written by the composer. Take note!
- Notice the *poco rit.* before the return of the rondo theme, in measures 20 and 48.
- Make the contrasting section at measure 32 louder and a bit faster for contrast.
- This brooding piece will take some practice over time to understand and master.

### Rondo-Toccata (No. 4)

*Practice and Performance Tips*

- The piece can create a brilliant impact in performance. Because the left hand remains in a contained position through much of it, it will sound more difficult than it is.
- Practice hands separately, slowly at first.
- Learn the articulation (*staccato* touch) from the beginning.
- Use the sustaining pedal only where explicitly indicated by Kabalevsky.
- Note the change of touch, moving from *staccato* to *legato* in measure 17.
- With the hands playing the same notes in octaves beginning in measure 19, make sure both right and left hands are playing exactly the same articulation.
- Practice tempo can increase as you master the music, but always maintain steadiness.
- Only play the piece as fast as you can manage in making it sound under control. Do not let it run away from you.

### Prelude and Fugue in G Major from *Preludes and Fugues*, Op. 61, No. 1

Composed 1958–59

*Practice and Performance Tips*

- Play the Prelude section with the care of a chorale, with rounded tone and with the top treble note only slightly brought out.
- Make sure all the notes of the chords sound exactly together in the prelude, and the harmonies are clear.
- Tasteful use of the sustaining pedal is needed for the prelude (and its reprise at the end). Make sure you carefully pedal to clarify the change of harmony.
- The fugue begins in measure 21.
- Practice each hand separately in the fugue.
- Use no sustaining pedal in the fugue.
- This fugue should be played very evenly and cleanly, in the spirit of a Baroque fugue.
- The trickiest spot comes with the crossing of the hands in measures 48–49. Prepare for this.
- Your tempo for the fugue should be determined by the tempo at which you can manage measures 48–49 gracefully.

### Naughty Boys from *Six Pieces (Children's Dreams)*, Op. 88, No. 6

composed 1971

*Practice and Performance Tips*

- Practice hands separately. If you learn the articulations as you learn the notes and rhythms, the piece will come together more easily.
- Notice the very specific pedaling, releasing the pedal on beat 2.
- The five-note scale must be played evenly.
- Emphasize the accents, slurs and syncopation in measures 24–27 and 35–38.
- By far the most challenging section is measures 39 to the end. You must prepare for the big leap in hand position.
- As with all Kabalevsky, every note has very specific articulation regarding accents and slurring. Do your best to do what the composer asks.
- After practicing slowly hands together, work up to a quicker tempo that can stay steady throughout. Choose the hardest part of the piece. How fast can you play this? That's your tempo for the entire piece.

—Richard Walters, editor

# Slow Waltz
## from *24 Pieces for Children*

Dmitri Kabalevsky
Op. 39, No. 23

# Prelude and Fugue in G Major
from *Preludes and Fugues*

Dmitri Kabalevsky
Op. 61, No. 1

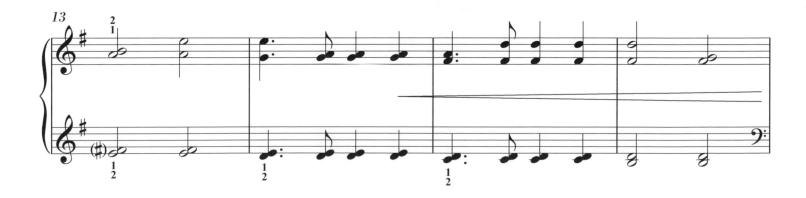

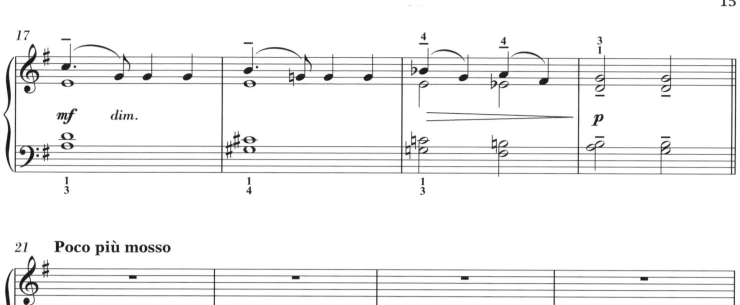

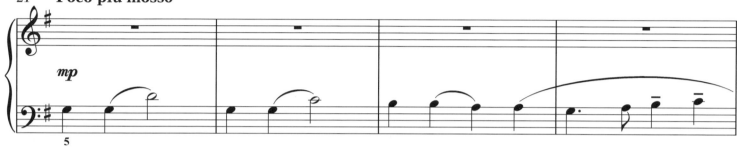

# Rondo-Toccata
## from *Four Rondos*

Dmitri Kabalevsky
Op. 60, No. 4

# Rondo-Song
## from *Four Rondos*

Dmitri Kabalevsky
Op. 60, No. 3

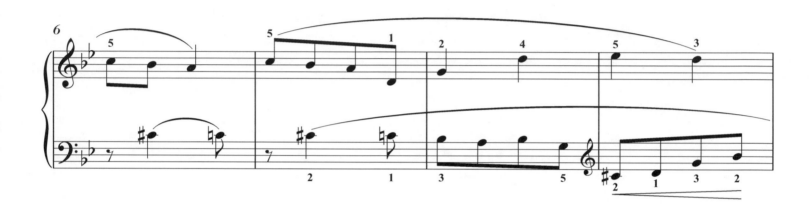

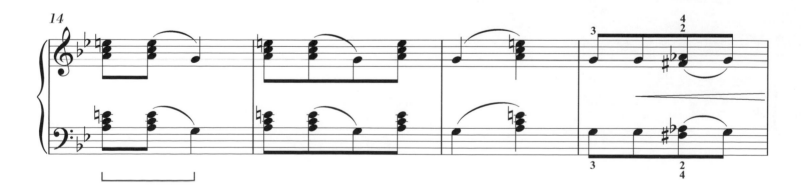

# Sporting Game

from *From Pioneer Life*

Dmitri Kabalevsky
Op. 14, No. 2

**Scherzando**

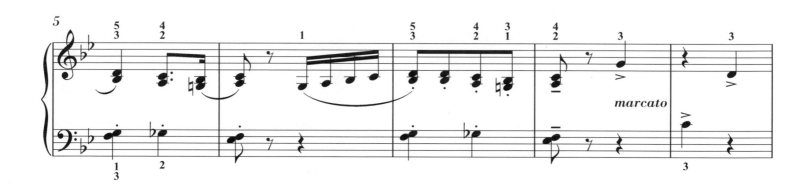

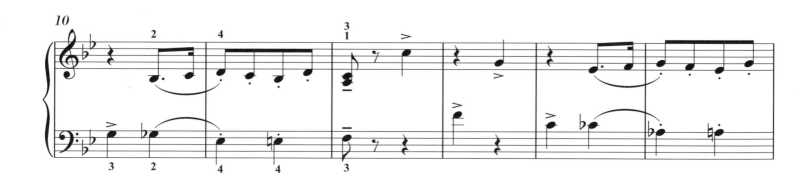

# Naughty Boys
## from *Six Pieces (Children's Dreams)*

Dmitri Kabalevsky
Op. 88, No. 6

# Etude in A minor
## from *30 Pieces for Children*

Dmitri Kabalevsky
Op. 27, No. 3

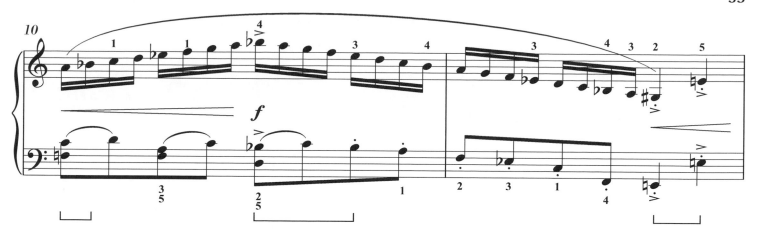

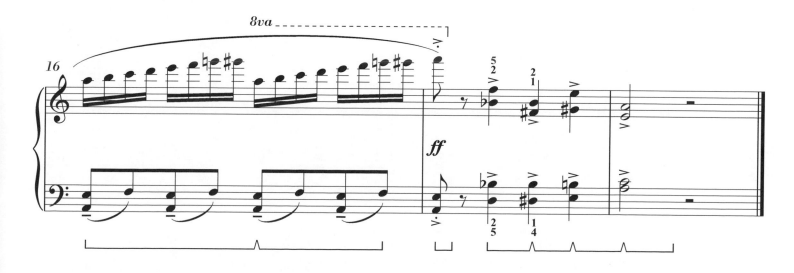

# A Little Prank

from *30 Pieces for Children*

Dmitri Kabalevsky
Op. 27, No. 13

# Dance Variations on a Russian Folk Song
## from *Five Easy Variations on Folk Themes*

Dmitri Kabalevsky
Op. 51, No. 2

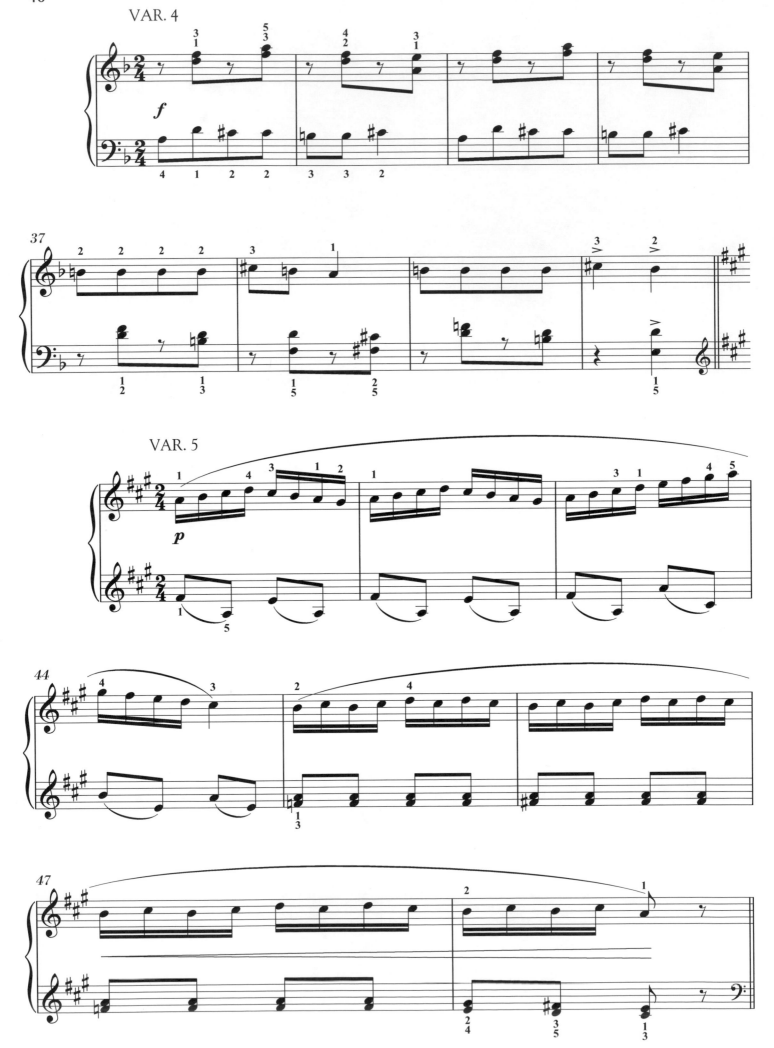

VAR. 6

# Novelette

from *30 Pieces for Children*

Dmitri Kabalevsky
Op. 27, No. 25

# Fairy Tale
## from *30 Pieces for Children*

Dmitri Kabalevsky
Op. 27, No. 20

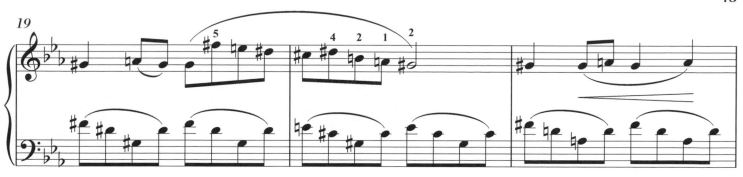

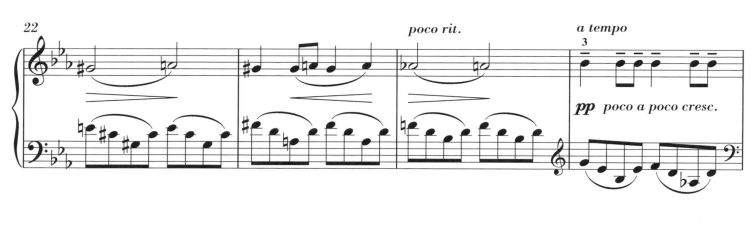

# Lyric Piece
## from *30 Pieces for Children*

Dmitri Kabalevsky
Op. 27, No. 16

**Andantino con moto** [♩ = c. 104]

# The Chase

from *30 Pieces for Children*

Dmitri Kabalevsky
Op. 27, No. 21

# Seven Cheerful Variations
# on a Slovakian Folk Song

from *Five Easy Variations on Folk Themes*

Dmitri Kabalevsky
Op. 51, No. 4

**THEME**

**Allegretto scherzando**

VAR. 1

VAR. 3

VAR. 4

VAR. 5

VAR. 6

VAR. 7 and CODA

# Prelude in D-flat Major

from *24 Preludes*

Dmitri Kabalevsky
Op. 38, No. 15

# Prelude in C Major
from *24 Preludes*

Dmitri Kabalevsky
Op. 38, No. 1

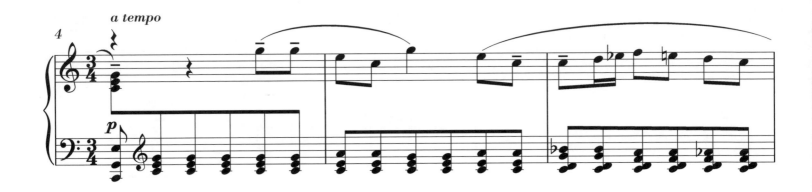

# Prelude in A minor

## from *Four Preludes*

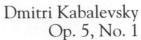

Dmitri Kabalevsky
Op. 5, No. 1

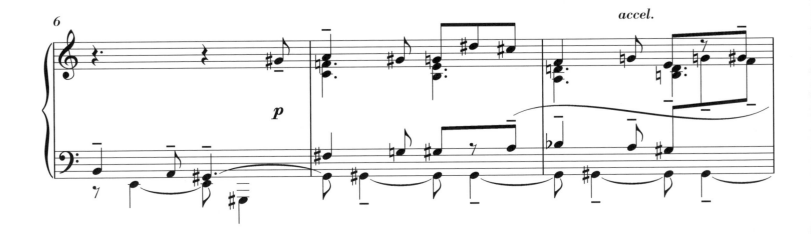